UNLOCK YOUR HIDDEN POTENTIAL

THE POWER OF SELF-DISCOVERY AND HOW TO ACCOMPLISH GREATER THINGS

ALFRED CURTIN

All Rights Reserved. Alfred Curtin 2024

No part of this publication should be reproduced, stored in a retrieval system, or transmitted in any form or by any means—electronic, mechanical, photocopying, recording, scanning, or otherwise—except as permitted without the prior written permission of the author.

TABLE OF CONTENT

INTRODUCTION 6

CHAPTER 1 10

MASTERING PERSONAL GROWTH 10

EMBRACING DISCOMFORT: NAVIGATING THROUGH THE CHALLENGES OF LEARNING 10

BECOMING HUMAN SPONGES: CULTIVATING THE ABILITY TO ABSORB AND ADAPT TO NEW INFORMATION 12

THE IMPERFECTIONISTS' APPROACH: FINDING BALANCE BETWEEN IMPERFECTION AND EXCELLENCE 15

CULTIVATING GRIT: DEVELOPING RESILIENCE IN THE FACE OF SETBACKS 19

CHAPTER 2 23

LIFELONG LEARNING AND CURIOSITY 23

MASTERING THE ART OF CONTINUOUS IMPROVEMENT . 23

CULTIVATING CURIOSITY: FOSTERING A LIFELONG LOVE FOR LEARNING AND GROWTH 26

STRUCTURES FOR MOTIVATION: BUILDING SUPPORT SYSTEMS TO OVERCOME OBSTACLES 30

MAKING THE DAILY GRIND EXCITING: INJECTING PASSION INTO ROUTINE TASKS 33

BREAKING THROUGH PLATEAUS: STRATEGIES FOR OVERCOMING STAGNATION AND GETTING UNSTUCK 37

CHAPTER 3 42

SELF-DETERMINATION AND HABITS 42

HARNESSING THE POWER OF SELF-DETERMINATION: TAKING CONTROL OF OUR DESTINY 42

BUILDING RESILIENT HABITS: ESTABLISHING ROUTINES THAT SUPPORT LONG-TERM SUCCESS 46

CULTIVATING A GROWTH MINDSET: EMBRACING CHALLENGES AND VIEWING FAILURE AS A STEPPING STONE TO SUCCESS 50

CHAPTER 4 55

CREATING OPPORTUNITIES 55

SYSTEMS OF OPPORTUNITY: ESTABLISHING CONDITIONS THAT ENCOURAGE DEVELOPMENT AND ACCOMPLISHMENT 55

RETHINKING EDUCATION: CREATING INSTITUTIONS THAT DEVELOP STUDENTS' UNIQUE SKILLS AND QUALITIES ... 58

THE UTILIZATION OF COLLECTIVE INTELLIGENCE: HARNESSING THE POTENTIAL OF COLLABORATIVE TEAMWORK 62

CHAPTER 5 67

IDENTIFYING AND FOSTERING TALENT 67

IDENTIFYING HIDDEN POTENTIAL: RECOGNIZING UNTAPPED TALENT DURING INTERVIEWS AND ACADEMIC ADMISSIONS 67

FOSTERING INCLUSIVITY: PROVIDING OPPORTUNITIES FOR EVERYONE TO THRIVE AND SUCCEED 71

BUILDING NETWORKS: CULTIVATING RELATIONSHIPS THAT OPEN DOORS TO NEW OPPORTUNITIES 75

CHAPTER 6 79

ADAPTABILITY AND RESILIENCE 79

EMBRACING CHANGE AND ADAPTABILITY NAVIGATING UNCERTAINTY WITH CONFIDENCE 79

THRIVING IN AMBIGUITY: DEVELOPING THE SKILLS TO NAVIGATE COMPLEX SITUATIONS 82

EMBRACING DIVERSITY: LEVERAGING DIFFERENCES FOR INNOVATION AND GROWTH 86

BUILDING RESILIENCE: BOUNCING BACK STRONGER FROM ADVERSITY 90

LEADING WITH EMPATHY: UNDERSTANDING AND VALUING DIFFERENT PERSPECTIVES 94

CONTINUOUSLY EVOLVING AND GROWING IN A RAPIDLY CHANGING WORLD 98

CONCLUSION 102

INTRODUCTION

Louis was a hardworking guy who was committed to his profession and his family, but he felt that something was missing in his life. He craved for a sense of purpose and fulfillment, but it seemed to elude him at every turn. While wandering via a neighborhood bookstore, Louis came upon this book, He picked up the book and started reading after being intrigued by the title. As Louis read the book, he discovered the value of understanding oneself, making significant goals, and embracing the road of personal development. Inspired by what he read, Louis determined to apply the book's lessons to his own life. He began by devoting time each day to self-reflection, journaling about his thoughts, emotions, and goals. He also began to establish his basic values and priorities, determining what was actually important to him in life. As Louis immersed himself in the book's lessons, he saw tiny changes inside himself. He felt a renewed feeling of clarity and purpose, as if he was finally beginning to realize his full potential. He began to follow his passions with newfound zeal, resuming hobbies and interests that had previously been abandoned. But arguably the most profound change occurred in Louis' thinking. He began to perceive challenges not as impediments, but as chances for growth and learning. He accepted failure as a natural part of the path and learned to come back stronger each time. Louis' life changed dramatically as the months and years passed. He discovered fulfillment in his career, joy in his relationships, and a sense of inner calm he had never experienced before. He had discovered his buried potential and was now living a life that truly reflected his deepest ambitions and aspirations. Reflecting on his path, Louis understood that he had always possessed the ability to transform his life. The book had simply functioned as a beacon of light, guiding him through the challenges of self-discovery and personal development. So, armed with the lessons he gained from his trip, Louis went out to inspire others to discover their latent potential and achieve greater success in their own lives. For he understood that each of us possesses the ability to create the life we truly desire—a life full of purpose, passion, and limitless opportunities.

In a world full of untapped prospects and unexplored potentials, the journey of self-discovery holds the key to unlocking our hidden talents and reaching new heights of achievement and fulfillment. Welcome to the book "Unlock Your Hidden Potential: The Power of Self-Discovery and How to Accomplish Greater Things."

In the pages that follow, we start on a transforming journey—one that goes beyond the commonplace and digs deeply into the realms of self-awareness, growth, and empowerment. For everyone of us has a pool of untapped potential waiting to be unleashed—potential that, once unlocked, may propel us toward our wildest hopes and desires.

But first, let us consider the essence of self-discovery. It is the process of peeling back the layers of our identities to reveal the complexities of our desires, passions, strengths, and shortcomings. It is about discovering who we truly are—beyond the masks we wear, the roles we perform, and the expectations set on us by society.

Self-discovery is a journey, punctuated by moments of clarity, insight, and revelation.

It is a path of introspection, inquiry, and self-reflection that leads us to discover our most profound truths, values, and desires.

As we embark on this journey together, let us recognize the potential of self-discovery as a driver of personal growth and transformation. Let us dare to peel back the layers of our identity, address our fears and doubts, and accept the entirety of who we are.

For within the depths of self-discovery lies the key to unlocking our hidden potential—the ability to accomplish more than we ever imagined imaginable. So let us go on this voyage with open hearts and minds, eager to explore the wide landscapes of our inner selves and realize the boundless potential that exists inside.

CHAPTER 1
MASTERING PERSONAL GROWTH

EMBRACING DISCOMFORT: NAVIGATING THROUGH THE CHALLENGES OF LEARNING

In the pursuit of personal and professional development, one of the most significant barriers individuals encounter is the distress associated with learning.

Learning, by its nature, necessitates venturing outside of one's comfort zone, grappling with uncertainty, and confronting unfamiliar challenges. However, embracing discomfort is essential for navigating through the challenges of learning and unearthing one's latent potential.

At its center, embracing distress involves a willingness to confront and embrace the unknown. It requires individuals to transcend the confines of familiarity and venture into uncharted territory. While the prospect of uncertainty can elicit feelings of dread and apprehension, it is also a fertile ground for development and discovery.

Embracing distress is not about seeking out hardship for its own sake, but rather recognizing that growth often occurs at the margins of one's comfort zone. It involves pressing past self-imposed limitations and embracing the inherent vulnerability that comes with learning something new. By confronting distress head-on, individuals expand their capacity for resilience, adaptability, and creativity.

Moreover, embracing discomfort requires a transformation in perspective from viewing challenges as obstacles to opportunities for growth.

Rather than avoiding discomfort, individuals approach it with a sense of inquiry and openness, recognizing that each challenge presents an opportunity to learn, evolve, and expand one's horizons.

Central to the process of embracing discomfort is the cultivation of self-awareness and mindfulness. Individuals learn to observe their thoughts and emotions without judgment, allowing them to navigate through distress with greater clarity and equanimity. By cultivating a sense of presence and acceptance, individuals can more effectively manage the inevitable ups and downs of the learning journey.

Furthermore, embracing distress involves embracing failure as an essential part of the learning process. Failure is not a sign of incompetence or inadequacy but rather an opportunity for reflection, development, and course correction. By reframing failure as a natural and necessary part of the learning journey, individuals can mitigate the dread of making errors and approach challenges with greater resilience and determination.

In addition, embracing distress entails searching out diverse perspectives and experiences that challenge one's assumptions and beliefs. By exposing oneself to various viewpoints and methods of thinking, individuals can broaden their understanding of the world and cultivate empathy and compassion towards others. Embracing discomfort is not just about personal development but also about nurturing a sense of interconnectedness and solidarity with others.

BECOMING HUMAN SPONGES: CULTIVATING THE ABILITY TO ABSORB AND ADAPT TO NEW INFORMATION

In the enormous ocean of knowledge and experiences, humans have the extraordinary ability to become sponges, absorbing and adapting to new information with astonishing agility. This capacity rests at the heart of our cognitive evolution, enabling us to continuously learn, develop, and evolve.

In the journey of self-discovery and personal development, refining this ability to assimilate and adapt becomes not just advantageous but essential.

Imagine the human mind as a sponge, porous and receptive to the surrounding environment.

Just as a sponge soaks up water, our minds soak up information from various sources - literature, conversations, observations, experiences, and even disasters. However, unlike a static object, the human mind possesses the remarkable ability to comprehend, integrate, and transmute this absorbed information into actionable knowledge and wisdom.

To cultivate this ability effectively, it's crucial to nurture a mindset of openness and inquiry. Being open means being receptive to new ideas, perspectives, and experiences without prejudice or preconceived notions. It involves embracing ambiguity and venturing out of comfort zones to investigate the unknown. Curiosity, on the other hand, motivates our desire to pursue knowledge and understanding. It ignites the spark of discovery and drives us to investigate deeper into subjects that stimulate our interest.

Moreover, cultivating critical thinking skills is fundamental to becoming effective human sponges. Critical thinking empowers us to analyze information objectively, discerning fact from opinion, and logic from fallacy. It prompts us to query assumptions, challenge beliefs, and seek evidence to support claims.

By refining our critical thinking skills, we become better equipped to sift through the immense sea of information, separating the valuable insights from the noise.

In addition to openness and critical thinking, cultivating a growth mindset is essential for unleashing our complete potential as human receptacles. A growth mindset, as coined by psychologist Carol Dweck, is the belief that abilities and intellect can be developed through dedication and effort. Embracing a growth mindset means viewing challenges as opportunities for development, and setbacks as stepping stones to success. It involves adopting the process of learning and embracing feedback as a means to develop continuously.

Furthermore, promoting a diverse and inclusive learning environment enriches our sponge-like ability to assimilate and adapt.

Exposing ourselves to a diversity of perspectives, cultures, and experiences broadens our understanding of the world and enhances our capacity for empathy and compassion. It allows us to see beyond our own biases and limitations, fostering creativity and innovation.

Ultimately, becoming human reservoirs is not just about acquiring knowledge for the sake of accumulation but about leveraging that knowledge to effect positive change in ourselves and the world around us. It's about applying what we learn to solve problems, surmount challenges, and create opportunities. By nurturing our ability to absorb and adapt, we uncover our latent potential and embark on a journey of self-discovery and personal development that knows no bounds.

THE IMPERFECTIONISTS' APPROACH: FINDING BALANCE BETWEEN IMPERFECTION AND EXCELLENCE

In the pursuit of excellence, there exists a paradoxical truth: the path to grandeur is often paved with imperfection. The Imperfectionists' Approach is a philosophy that embraces the inherent disorder of the human experience while striving for excellence.

It is about finding the balance between the pursuit of perfection and the acceptance of imperfection, recognizing that true development and fulfillment reside in the space between the two extremes.

At its center, the Imperfectionists' Approach is rooted in self-compassion and self-acceptance. It acknowledges that excellence is an unattainable ideal and that striving for it can lead to feelings of frustration, inadequacy, and exhaustion. Instead of pursuing an impossible standard, individuals who embrace the Imperfectionists' Approach learn to accept themselves—including their flaws, errors, and shortcomings—with compassion and understanding.

Moreover, the Imperfectionists' Approach encourages individuals to embrace failure as an essential part of the learning process. Rather than dreading failure or perceiving it as a reflection of their worth, Imperfectionists see it as an opportunity for growth and self-discovery. They realize that failure is not the end of the road but rather a launching stone on the path to success. By reframing failure as a natural and necessary part of the journey, individuals can cultivate resilience, perseverance, and a growth mindset.

Furthermore, the Imperfectionists' Approach prioritizes progress over perfection. Rather than fixating on faultless outcomes, Imperfectionists focus on continuous refinement and iteration.

They realize that excellence is not achieved instantaneously but is the result of consistent effort, experimentation, and refinement over time. By embracing an iterative approach to development, individuals can break free from the paralyzing grasp of perfectionism and make meaningful progress toward their objectives.

In addition, the Imperfectionists' Approach fosters a culture of creativity and innovation. Imperfectionists understand that creativity flourishes in an environment where experimentation is encouraged, failure is tolerated, and diversity of thought is celebrated. By embracing imperfection as a catalyst for innovation, individuals can unleash their creativity and explore new possibilities beyond the constraints of perfectionism.

Moreover, the Imperfectionists' Approach emphasizes the importance of balance in all aspects of existence.

While striving for excellence is admirable, it should not come at the expense of one's well-being, relationships, or sense of fulfillment. Imperfectionists comprehend that true success is multidimensional, encompassing not only professional achievements but also personal development, health, happiness, and meaningful connections with others. By prioritizing balance and harmony in their lives, individuals can unlock their latent potential and accomplish greater things with authenticity and integrity.

The Imperfectionists' Approach offers a refreshing perspective on the pursuit of excellence—one that embraces imperfection as a natural and essential part of the human experience. By cultivating self-compassion, embracing failure, prioritizing progress over perfection, fostering creativity and innovation, and pursuing balance in all aspects of life, individuals can unlock their latent potential and achieve fulfillment on their own terms.

CULTIVATING GRIT: DEVELOPING RESILIENCE IN THE FACE OF SETBACKS

Grit is a critical attribute that must be cultivated in order to effectively unlock our latent potential. Grit is the fortitude and determination to continue making progress in the face of setbacks, impediments, and challenges. Inner fortitude enables us to maintain our concentration on objectives, adjust to challenges, and ultimately accomplish more. This segment will delve into the significance of nurturing fortitude and methodologies for constructing resilience when confronted with obstacles.

Fundamentally, grit entails adopting a growth mindset—the conviction that one's capabilities and intellect are susceptible to enhancement via diligence and exertion. Adopting this perspective allows us to perceive obstacles as chances for personal development rather than formidable impediments. According to research conducted by psychologist Angela Duckworth, fortitude is a more accurate predictor of success than intelligence or aptitude alone. Achieving mastery and success ultimately requires a determination to persist in the face of obstacles.

By accepting failure as an inherent component of the learning process, one can initiate the development of fortitude. Instead of dreading failure, we can reframe it as feedback that provides valuable insights into what works and what doesn't. Thomas Edison famously said, "I have not faltered. I've just discovered 10,000 methods that won't work." By adopting this perspective, we can approach setbacks with curiosity and resilience, seeing them as opportunities to learn and develop.

Another aspect of developing grit is setting distinct objectives and maintaining a sense of purpose.

When we have a compelling vision of what we want to achieve, it becomes simpler to remain motivated and resilient in the face of challenges.

Research has shown that individuals who have a strong sense of purpose are better able to surmount obstacles and persevere through difficult times. By aligning our actions with our values and aspirations, we can draw into a profound reservoir of inner strength that propels us forward.

In addition to having a growth mindset and a sense of purpose, building grit also requires cultivating self-discipline and perseverance.

This means developing habits and routines that support our objectives, even when it's difficult or inconvenient. It involves making modest, consistent endeavors towards our objectives, day in and day out, regardless of external circumstances. As we build momentum and see progress, our confidence and resilience develop, reinforcing our commitment to our journey.

Furthermore, building a support network of mentors, colleagues, and acquaintances can provide invaluable encouragement and guidance along the way.

Surrounding ourselves with people who believe in our potential and offer constructive feedback can help us stay motivated and resilient, particularly during challenging times. By seeking support from others and learning from their experiences, we can obtain new perspectives and insights that stimulate our growth and development.

Ultimately, cultivating fortitude is a lifelong endeavor that requires dedication, resilience, and perseverance. It's about embracing challenges as opportunities for growth, remaining focused on our objectives, and never giving up, even when the going gets tough. By developing fortitude, we uncover our latent potential and empower ourselves to accomplish greater things than we ever imagined possible. So, let's embrace the journey, confront adversity with courage, and unleash the power within us to attain our ambitions.

CHAPTER 2

LIFELONG LEARNING AND CURIOSITY

MASTERING THE ART OF CONTINUOUS IMPROVEMENT

When striving for personal and professional development, organizations and individuals have consistently been guided to excellence by the immutable principle of continuous improvement. Mastering the art of continuous development fundamentally requires an unwavering dedication to ongoing education, adjustment, and enhancement. This philosophy posits that despite their considerable expertise, organizations and individuals alike are perpetually capable of making progress, introducing novel ideas, and undergoing evolution.

At the core of the notion of continuous development lies the understanding that stagnation is diametrically opposed to advancement. Through the adoption of a paradigm centered on perpetual enhancement, individuals initiate a process of introspection, self-exploration, and personal mastery.

They recognize that every experience, regardless of success or failure, offers a chance for personal and professional advancement. Instead of being deterred by obstacles, they perceive them as opportunities to develop their skills and fortitude.

Fundamentally, attaining proficiency in the field of continuous improvement entails nurturing a collection of cornerstone principles and methodologies that nurture development and distinction. These principles comprise an all-encompassing strategy for both personal and professional growth, taking into account multiple facets including mental, emotional, physical, and spiritual wellness.

One of the fundamental principles of continuous improvement is the pursuit of excellence through unremitting self-assessment and feedback. Those dedicated to ongoing development proactively solicit feedback from mentors, peers, and stakeholders, perceiving it as a critical input for personal growth. They recognize that honest feedback, whether positive or constructive, functions as a catalyst for development and refinement.

Moreover, mastering continuous improvement involves a dedication to lifelong learning and skill development.

Individuals cultivate a growth mindset, embracing challenges and setbacks as opportunities to acquire new knowledge, skills, and competencies. They invest time and resources in personal and professional development, whether through formal education, training programs, or self-directed learning initiatives.

Another essential aspect of continuous development is the cultivation of resilience and adaptability. Individuals realize that change is inevitable and embrace it as a catalyst for growth and innovation. They develop the capacity to navigate uncertainty and ambiguity with grace and resilience, leveraging challenges as opportunities for personal and professional transformation.

Furthermore, mastering continuous development requires a commitment to innovation and creativity. Individuals challenge the status quo, investigate new ideas, and experiment with novel approaches to problem-solving. They cultivate a culture of innovation within themselves and their organizations, encouraging curiosity, experimentation, and collaboration.

Integral to the voyage of continuous development is the cultivation of mindfulness and self-awareness.

Individuals develop a thorough comprehension of their strengths, weaknesses, values, and aspirations, enabling them to make intentional choices aligned with their authentic selves. They prioritize self-care and well-being, recognizing that sustainable development necessitates a balance between ambition and self-care.

Mastering the art of continuous improvement is a transformative voyage that empowers individuals to uncover their hidden potential and accomplish greater things. It is a voyage characterized by curiosity, resilience, and a relentless commitment to excellence. By embracing the principles and practices of continuous improvement, individuals can unleash their inherent talents, surmount challenges, and create a meaningful impact in their lives and the world around them.

CULTIVATING CURIOSITY: FOSTERING A LIFELONG LOVE FOR LEARNING AND GROWTH

Curiosity is the spark that ignites the flame of self-discovery and propels us toward unleashing our inactive potential. It is the urgency to investigate novel concepts, the insatiable desire for knowledge, and the willingness to accept uncertainty.

This section will explore the significance of nurturing inquiry and tactics for promoting an enduring passion for knowledge acquisition and personal development.

Curiosity, as a fundamental characteristic of the human species, propels individuals to pursue comprehension and construct meaning from their surroundings. We are naturally inquisitive creatures from an early age, perpetually seeking novel experiences, experimenting, and posing inquiries. However, as we grow older, our intrinsic curiosity can be dampened by societal norms, the dread of failure, and the pressures of conformity. It is critical to reignite this sense of awe and inquiry in order to commence a voyage of self-exploration and the revelation of our latent capabilities.

To foster inquiry, one must initially develop a growth mindset—the conviction that one's capabilities and intellect are capable of progression with diligence and sustained effort. Adopting a "yet" mentality, embracing challenges, and viewing failures as learning opportunities are all aspects of this mindset. We say "I cannot do this yet" rather than "I am unable to do this." A mere change in perspective fosters an abundance of opportunities and motivates us to approach existence with inquisitiveness and eagerness.

Moreover, cultivating inquiry requires the establishment of an atmosphere that encourages investigation and revelation. This involves exposing ourselves to diverse perspectives, ideas, and experiences, both within and outside our comfort zones. Whether it's traveling to new places, perusing books on unfamiliar topics, or engaging in thought-provoking conversations, every opportunity to learn is an opportunity to stimulate our curiosity and expand our horizons.

Moreover, embracing ambiguity and embracing the unexpected is essential for cultivating curiosity. Instead of fearing the unfamiliar, we can approach it with a sense of wonder and enthusiasm, seeing it as an opportunity for development and discovery. As Albert Einstein famously said, "The important point is not to cease questioning. Curiosity has its own cause for existing." By embracing ambiguity and embracing the unknown, we can unleash our curiosity and tap into our latent potential.

Furthermore, fostering a lifelong passion for learning requires developing habits and routines that prioritize curiosity and growth. This means carving out time for self-directed exploration, whether it's through literature, attending workshops, or pursuing hobbies and interests.

By making learning a priority in our daily lives, we not only expand our knowledge and abilities but also cultivate a sense of fulfillment and purpose.

In addition to individual efforts, cultivating curiosity also requires creating supportive environments that encourage exploration and innovation. This includes promoting a culture of curiosity in schools, workplaces, and communities, where asking questions, challenging assumptions, and experimenting are celebrated and encouraged. By nurturing a culture of curiosity, we create spaces where individuals feel empowered to investigate their interests, unleash their creativity, and unlock their latent potential.

Furthermore, fostering inquiry also involves cultivating a sense of amazement and awe for the world around us. Whether it's marveling at the beauty of nature, contemplating the intricacies of the universe, or pondering on the complexity of the human mind, cultivating a sense of awe opens our hearts and minds to new possibilities and stimulates our curiosity and creativity.

By embracing the wonder of life, we awaken to the infinite possibilities that exist within and around us, inspiring us to embark on a voyage of self-discovery and development. Ultimately, cultivating curiosity is a lifelong voyage that requires dedication, fortitude, and an open heart and mind. It's about embracing the unknown, asking questions, and pursuing understanding, even when the answers are elusive. By cultivating curiosity, we unlock our latent potential, expand our horizons, and embark on a journey of self-discovery and development that enriches our lives and empowers us to accomplish greater things than we ever imagined possible. So, let's embrace the marvel of life, cultivate our curiosity, and liberate the power within us to create a brighter, more fulfilling future.

STRUCTURES FOR MOTIVATION: BUILDING SUPPORT SYSTEMS TO OVERCOME OBSTACLES

In the journey of unleashing our latent potential, we often encounter obstacles that challenge our resolve and test our determination. Whether it's self-doubt, fear of failure, or external barriers, navigating these challenges requires more than just individual effort—it requires a strong support system and structures for motivation to keep us moving forward. In this introductory section, we'll examine the importance of building support systems and structures for motivation to overcome obstacles and achieve our objectives.

Self-discovery is a transformative journey that invites us to investigate the depths of our being, uncover our strengths and limitations, and realize our true potential. It's a journey of introspection and reflection, where we confront our fears, insecurities, and limiting beliefs, and cultivate a deeper understanding of ourselves. However, the path to self-discovery is not always straightforward travel. Along the journey, we encounter obstacles and challenges that threaten to disrupt our progress and dampen our spirits.

One of the most common obstacles we face on the journey of self-discovery is self-doubt. It's the nagging voice in our mind that tells us we're not good enough, smart enough, or talented enough to achieve our objectives. Left unchecked, self-doubt can erode our confidence and paralyze us with dread, preventing us from taking the necessary steps toward personal development and fulfillment. Overcoming self-doubt requires more than just positive thinking—it requires a supportive environment and structures for motivation that reinforce our confidence and keep us focused on our goals.

Another obstacle that often stands in the way of self-discovery is the dread of failure. It's the apprehension of falling short, making errors, and confronting rejection or criticism from others. The dread of failure can be debilitating, causing us to play it safe and avoid taking risks that could lead to growth and success.

To overcome this obstacle, we need a support system that provides encouragement, reassurance, and constructive feedback, enabling us to confront our fears head-on and persevere in the face of adversity.

External barriers, such as lack of resources, time constraints, or competing priorities, can also hinder our progress on the voyage of self-discovery. Without the necessary support and structures in place, these obstacles can seem insurmountable, leaving us feeling overburdened and demotivated. Building a support system that provides practical assistance, guidance, and accountability can help us navigate these challenges more effectively and stay on course toward attaining our objectives.

Creating structures for motivation is essential for overcoming obstacles and remaining focused on our journey of self-discovery. These structures provide the framework and support we need to maintain momentum, remain accountable, and surmount setbacks along the way. Whether it's setting SMART goals, creating a vision board, or establishing a daily routine, having clear objectives and actionable actions keeps us motivated and on track toward realizing our maximum potential.

Moreover, surrounding ourselves with a supportive network of friends, family, mentors, and colleagues can provide invaluable encouragement, inspiration, and guidance on our voyage. These individuals serve as cheerleaders, sounding boards, and accountability companions, helping us remain motivated and resilient in the face of adversity. By nurturing these relationships and seeking support when required, we can surmount obstacles more effectively and achieve our objectives with greater

MAKING THE DAILY GRIND EXCITING: INJECTING PASSION INTO ROUTINE TASKS

Life is filled with routine duties that can often feel mundane and uninspiring. From daily duties to repetitive work assignments, the monotony of the daily routine can drain our energy and dampen our spirits. However, what if there was a method to infuse passion and enthusiasm into even the most routine tasks? In this section, we'll investigate strategies for making the daily grind exciting and converting mundane activities into opportunities for self-discovery and personal development.

The daily grind incorporates the routine activities and obligations that make up our day-to-day existence. From waking up and getting ready for work to completing household duties and conducting errands, these tasks can feel like a never-ending treadmill of monotony. However, it's often within the routine of daily life that we have the greatest potential for self-discovery and personal development.

One of the secrets to making the daily routine exciting is to cultivate a mindset of curiosity and creativity. Instead of viewing routine tasks as duties to be marked off a list, we can approach them with a sense of wonder and exploration. Whether it's trying out a new recipe while cooking dinner or listening to an educational podcast while doing domestic tasks, finding ways to infuse novelty and stimulation into routine activities can make them more enjoyable and fulfilling.

Moreover, finding purpose and meaning in the tasks we perform can also make the daily drudgery more thrilling. Instead of focusing solely on the final result, we can transfer our attention to the process itself and the impact it has on our lives and the lives of others.

Whether it's contributing to a larger objective at work or creating a nurturing environment at home, finding significance in the duties we perform can infuse them with a sense of purpose and passion.

Furthermore, cultivating mindfulness and presence can transform routine tasks into opportunities for self-discovery and personal development. Instead of going through the routines of automation, we can cultivate awareness and attentiveness to the present moment. Whether it's relishing the flavor and texture of each mouthful while consuming breakfast or observing the sights and noises of nature while going for a walk, being fully present at the moment can enrich even the most mundane activities.

In addition to cultivating a mindset of curiosity, finding purpose, and embracing mindfulness, incorporating elements of play and creativity into routine duties can make them more pleasurable and thrilling. Whether it's listening to upbeat music while tidying the house or turning a work assignment into a game or challenge, finding ways to make duties more playful and creative can rekindle our sense of pleasure and enthusiasm.

Moreover, breaking duties down into smaller, more manageable stages can make them feel less daunting and more achievable. By setting realistic objectives and celebrating minor victories along the way, we can maintain momentum and stay motivated to tackle even the most challenging tasks. Additionally, incorporating pauses and rewards into our routine can provide much-needed moments of rest and rejuvenation, allowing us to return to our tasks with renewed energy and focus.

Making the daily grind thrilling is not about escaping from routine duties but rather embracing them as opportunities for self-discovery and personal development. By cultivating a mindset of curiosity, finding purpose, embracing mindfulness, incorporating play and creativity, and breaking tasks down into smaller stages, we can infuse even the most mundane activities with passion and enthusiasm. In the following chapters, we'll investigate in more detail the strategies and techniques for making the daily grind exciting and unleashing our latent potential in the process. So, let's embark on this voyage together and uncover the joy and fulfillment that can be found in the everyday moments of life.

BREAKING THROUGH PLATEAUS: STRATEGIES FOR OVERCOMING STAGNATION AND GETTING UNSTUCK

Plateaus are natural phases in our voyage of self-discovery and personal development. They occur when our progress levels off, and we find ourselves trapped in a quagmire, unable to move forward. Whether it's striking a roadblock in our occupations, feeling stagnant in our personal development, or experiencing a lack of motivation in pursuing our objectives, plateaus can be frustrating and disheartening. However, they also present an opportunity for reflection, reevaluation, and renewed determination. In this section, we'll investigate strategies for overcoming stagnation and getting resolved.

1. Self-Reflection and Awareness: The first step in overcoming plateaus is to pause and reflect on our current circumstances. This involves taking an honest inventory of our thoughts, emotions, and behaviors to identify any underlying causes of stagnation. Are there any limiting beliefs holding us back? Have we become complacent or lost sight of our goals? By cultivating self-awareness and obtaining insight into our patterns of behavior, we can begin to unravel the fundamental causes of our stagnation and pave the way for meaningful change.
2. Set New Goals and Challenges: Plateaus often occur when we become too content or complacent with our current level of achievement. To break through stagnation, it's essential to set new objectives and challenges that extend us beyond our comfort zone. This could entail pursuing a new talent or hobby, taking on a leadership role at work, or establishing ambitious targets for personal development. By setting clear objectives and challenging ourselves to develop, we can reignite our passion and motivation for self-discovery and accomplishment.

3. Seek Inspiration and Learning: Sometimes, all it takes to break through a plateau is a fresh perspective or a surge of inspiration. Seek out sources of inspiration that resonate with you, whether it's reading books, listening to podcasts, attending seminars, or communicating with mentors and peers who have overcome similar challenges. By exposing ourselves to new ideas and perspectives, we can reignite our curiosity and enthusiasm for development and discovery.
4. Embrace Failure and Learn from Setbacks: Plateaus often occur as a result of fear of failure or a reluctance to take risks. However, failure is an inevitable part of the voyage of self-discovery and personal development. Instead of dreading failure, embrace it as a valuable learning opportunity. Reflect on past setbacks and errors, extract the lessons learned, and use them to inform your future actions. By reframing failure as a stepping stone to success, you can surmount the dread of stagnation and embrace the journey of growth with courage and resilience.
5. Practice Self-Compassion and Patience: Overcoming plateaus takes time and effort, and it's vital to be kind to

yourself along the way. Practice self-compassion and forbearance as you navigate through challenges and setbacks. Celebrate small victories and progress, even if they seem insignificant. Remember that growth is a gradual process, and every step forward, no matter how minor, brings you closer to unlocking your latent potential.

6. Create a Support System: Surround yourself with a supportive network of friends, family, mentors, and colleagues who can provide encouragement, guidance, and accountability. Share your objectives and challenges with them, and depend on them for support when you're feeling stuck or discouraged. Having a strong support system can provide the motivation and reassurance you need to push through plateaus and continue on your journey of self-discovery and accomplishment.

7. Take Action and Stay Consistent: Finally, the most essential strategy for overcoming plateaus is to take action and stay consistent in your efforts. Break down your objectives into smaller, manageable steps, and commit to taking consistent action toward attaining them. Even on days when you feel unmotivated or

uninspired, challenge yourself to take modest, incremental steps forward. By remaining committed and persevering through challenges, you can overcome plateaus and unleash your hidden potential.

Plateaus are a natural part of the journey of self-discovery and personal development, but they don't have to be perpetual. By cultivating self-awareness, setting new objectives, pursuing inspiration, embracing failure, practicing self-compassion, creating a support system, and taking consistent action, you can overcome stagnation and get unstuck. Remember that growth is a lifelong endeavor, and every challenge you surmount brings you one step closer to unlocking your hidden potential and attaining greater things. So, embrace the voyage, remain resilient, and keep moving forward with courage and determination.

CHAPTER 3

SELF-DETERMINATION AND HABITS

HARNESSING THE POWER OF SELF-DETERMINATION: TAKING CONTROL OF OUR DESTINY

Self-determination is the motivating force behind our ability to shape our own destinies. It's the inner strength and conviction that empowers us to take control of our lives, set meaningful objectives, and pursue our ambitions with unwavering determination. In this section, we'll investigate the significance of harnessing the power of self-determination and strategies for taking control of our destinies.

1. Elucidate Your Vision: The first step in utilizing the power of self-determination is to elucidate your vision for the future.

Take the time to reflect on what genuinely matters to you and what you want to achieve in life. Set distinct, specific objectives that align with your values and aspirations. By having a clear vision of what you want to accomplish, you can remain focused and motivated on your journey of self-discovery and personal development.

2. Cultivate Self-Belief: Self-determination necessitates a strong sense of self-belief and conviction in your abilities. Cultivate a positive mindset and believe in your potential to surmount obstacles and achieve your objectives. Challenge negative self-talk and limiting beliefs that hold you back, and replace them with affirmations and positive affirmations that reinforce your confidence and self-worth.

3. Take Responsibility for Your Actions: Self-determination involves assuming complete responsibility for your actions and decisions. Instead of blaming external circumstances or other people for your setbacks, accept ownership of your choices and learn from your errors. Recognize that you have the power to influence your own destiny through the actions you take each day. By assuming responsibility for your actions, you empower yourself to create the existence you desire.

4. Set SMART Goals: To leverage the power of self-determination, it's essential to set SMART goals—

specific, measurable, achievable, pertinent, and time-bound. Break down your objectives into smaller, actionable steps, and construct a plan for achieving them. Regularly review your progress and make adjustments as required to stay on track. By setting SMART goals, you construct a roadmap for success and empower yourself to take decisive action towards your aspirations.

5. Persist in the Face of Adversity: Self-determination requires resilience and perseverance in the face of adversity. Understand that setbacks and challenges are a natural part of the journey towards success, and use them as opportunities for development and learning. Stay resilient in the face of obstacles, and keep pressing forward towards your goals, even when the going gets difficult. By maintaining a steadfast commitment to your ambitions, you can surmount any obstacle and achieve greatness.

6. Seek Support and Accountability: Surround yourself with a supportive network of friends, family, mentors, and colleagues who can provide encouragement, guidance, and accountability. Share your goals and

aspirations with them, and depend on them for support when you're feeling discouraged or overburdened. Having a strong support system can help you remain motivated and focused on your journey of self-determination.

7. Celebrate Your Successes: Finally, celebrate your successes along the path to utilizing the power of self-determination. Acknowledge your achievements, no matter how minor, and take pride in the progress you've made towards your objectives. Celebrating your successes reinforces your confidence and motivation, and motivates your determination to continue striving for excellence.

Harnessing the power of self-determination is essential for taking control of our destinies and unleashing our latent potential. By clarifying your vision, cultivating self-belief, taking responsibility for your actions, setting SMART objectives, persisting in the face of adversity, seeking support and accountability, and celebrating your successes, you can empower yourself to create the life you desire. Remember that you have the power to shape your own destiny, and with determination and perseverance, you can accomplish anything you set your mind to. So, embrace the journey of self-discovery and personal development, and take control of your destiny with courage and conviction.

BUILDING RESILIENT HABITS: ESTABLISHING ROUTINES THAT SUPPORT LONG-TERM SUCCESS

In the pursuit of unleashing our latent potential and attaining our goals, one of the most effective tools at our disposal is the establishment of resilient routines. Habits form the foundation of our daily existence, influencing our behaviors, actions, and ultimately, our outcomes. By intentionally cultivating resilient habits, we can create routines that support long-term success and impel us forward on our voyage of self-discovery and personal development. In this section, we'll examine the significance of developing resilient habits and strategies for establishing routines that contribute to greater fulfillment and accomplishment.

1. Identify Your Values and Priorities: The first step in developing resilient behaviors is to identify your values and priorities. What matters most to you? What do you want to accomplish in life? By clarifying your values and priorities, you can align your behaviors and routines with your long-

term goals and aspirations. For example, if health and fitness are essential to you, establishing a habit of regular exercise and nutritious nutrition can support your overall well-being and longevity.

2. Start modest and Be Consistent: When it comes to developing resilient behaviors, starting modest and being consistent is essential. Instead of attempting to overhaul your entire life overnight, concentrate on making small, incremental adjustments to your daily routines. Start with one habit at a time, and commit to practicing it consistently until it becomes automatic. Whether it's rising up early, meditating for five minutes, or reading for 20 minutes before bed, consistency is the key to success.

3. Create Trigger and Reward Systems: To reinforce resilient habits, create trigger and reward systems that help reinforce positive behaviors. A trigger is a cue or reminder that prompts you to engage in a specific habit, while a reward is a positive reinforcement that reinforces the behavior. For example, if you want to establish a habit of journaling every evening, you could use a stimulus such as setting an alarm on your phone, and reward yourself with a cup of tea or a

relaxing bath after you've completed your journaling session.

4. Practice Self-Discipline and Accountability: Building resilient behaviors requires self-discipline and accountability. Set explicit objectives for yourself and hold yourself accountable for following through on your commitments. You can also enlist the support of a friend, family member, or mentor to help keep you accountable and provide encouragement along the path. By practicing self-discipline and accountability, you can remain focused and motivated to adhere to your practices, even when confronted with challenges or setbacks.

5. Adapt and Adjust as Needed: Resilient behaviors are flexible and adaptable to changing circumstances. As you progress on your journey of self-discovery and personal development, be prepared to alter and modify your routines as needed. If you find that a particular habit isn't serving you well or isn't aligned with your values and priorities, don't be afraid to let it go and replace it with a more beneficial one. Remember that the objective is not perfection, but progress.

6. Practice Self-Care and Rest: Building resilient routines requires energy and commitment, which is why it's essential to prioritize self-care and rest.

Make time for activities that recharge and rejuvenate you, such as exercise, meditation, or spending time with loved ones. Get plenty of sleep and take pauses when needed to avoid fatigue and maintain your motivation and focus. Remember that taking care of yourself is essential for developing resilient habits and achieving long-term success.

7. Celebrate Your Progress: Finally, celebrate your progress and accomplishments along the road. Building resilient behaviors is a journey, not a destination, and every move forward, no matter how minor, deserves recognition and celebration. Acknowledge your successes and milestones, and use them as motivation to keep pressing forward on your path to unleashing your latent potential and attaining greater things.

Developing resilient habits is essential for establishing routines that support long-term success and fulfillment. By identifying your values and priorities, starting small and being consistent, creating trigger and reward systems, practicing self-discipline and accountability, adapting and adjusting as needed, prioritizing self-care and rest, and celebrating your progress, you can create habits that propel you forward on your journey of self-discovery and personal growth. So, embrace the power of resilient routines, and uncover your latent potential with intentionality, perseverance, and commitment.

CULTIVATING A GROWTH MINDSET: EMBRACING CHALLENGES AND VIEWING FAILURE AS A STEPPING STONE TO SUCCESS

The development of a growth mindset—the core conviction that our skills and intelligence can be enhanced by commitment and effort—is essential to realizing our hidden potential. This kind of thinking enables us to rise to the occasion, keep going after failures, and see failure as a priceless chance for development. This section will discuss the value of developing a growth mindset, as well as methods for accepting obstacles and using setbacks as stepping stones to success.

Accepting Difficulties:

The first step in developing a growth mindset is to see obstacles as chances for personal development. When faced with obstacles, people with a growth mindset see them as opportunities to grow and stretch themselves rather than as something to avoid or run away from.

They are aware that taking on obstacles head-on is crucial for both career and personal growth.

By accepting difficulties, we force ourselves to step outside of our comfort zones and into new areas of development and exploration. Whatever the obstacle, it may be taking on a challenging project at work, picking up a new skill, or facing a personal fear; all of these offer chances to push ourselves to the edge, become more resilient, and discover new possibilities. Through reinterpreting obstacles as chances for development, we can transcend self-imposed constraints and reveal our latent capabilities.

Seeing Setbacks as a Prelude to Achievement:

Developing a growth mindset includes accepting obstacles as well as seeing failure as an inevitable and essential part of learning. Growth-minded people perceive failure as just feedback that offers insightful information about what works and what doesn't, as opposed to dreading it or viewing it as a reflection of their talents. Instead of viewing failure as a barrier that must be overcome at all costs, they view it as a stepping stone to success.

We respond to setbacks and disappointments in a more positive and resilient way when we see failure as a necessary step on the path to success. Rather than moping over our errors or giving up in the face of difficulty, we view failure as a chance to get better. We evaluate what went wrong, pinpoint opportunities for development, and modify our strategy as necessary. We become more resilient, adaptive, and driven in our pursuit of our goals when we accept failure as a normal part of the path to success.

Methods for Fostering a Growth Mentality:

Practice Self-Compassion: Having self-compassion, or the capacity to be kind and understanding to oneself, particularly when confronted with failure or setbacks, is essential to developing a growth mentality. By appreciating our efforts, accepting responsibility for our errors, and treating ourselves with the same compassion and understanding that we would extend to a friend, we can cultivate self-compassion rather than punishing ourselves for our inadequacies.

Challenge Negative Self-Talk: By boosting limiting beliefs and undermining our confidence, negative self-talk can hinder our efforts to develop a growth mindset.

We can confront our inner critic and overcome negative self-talk by reframing setbacks as chances for growth and substituting positive affirmations for negative ideas. By cultivating a more positive and empowering inner dialogue, we can strengthen our belief in our ability to learn and grow.

Seek Feedback and Support: Seeking feedback and support from others is essential for cultivating a growth mindset. Positive criticism can help us identify our areas of strength and growth, and encouragement from friends, family, and mentors can boost our self-esteem and drive. By surrounding ourselves with a supportive network of individuals who believe in our potential, we can stay motivated and resilient in the face of challenges and setbacks.

Celebrate Progress and Effort: Cultivating a growth mindset involves celebrating progress and effort, rather than focusing solely on outcomes. Instead of measuring success solely by achievements or milestones, we can celebrate the progress we've made and the effort we've invested in our goals. By acknowledging our efforts and progress, we reinforce our belief in our ability to learn and grow, regardless of the outcome.

Stay Curious and Open-Minded: Finally, cultivating a growth mindset requires staying curious and open-minded to new experiences, ideas, and perspectives. Instead of clinging to fixed beliefs or assumptions, we can approach life with a sense of curiosity and wonder, eager to learn and grow from every opportunity. By maintaining an open mind and embracing new challenges with enthusiasm, we can continue to expand our horizons and unlock our hidden potential.

CHAPTER 4

CREATING OPPORTUNITIES

SYSTEMS OF OPPORTUNITY: ESTABLISHING CONDITIONS THAT ENCOURAGE DEVELOPMENT AND ACCOMPLISHMENT

First of all,

The surroundings we live in have a significant impact on the experiences and results we have while on our path of self-discovery and personal development. The environments, customs, and ecosystems that foster development, education, and success are known as systems of opportunity. We may reach our full potential and do things we never would have imagined by establishing surroundings that encourage development and uphold our goals.

These opportunity systems can be found in a variety of settings, such as social networks, businesses, and educational institutions. They are distinguished by their dedication to fostering an environment of development, creativity, and cooperation where people are inspired to follow their passions, explore their interests, and push themselves to new limits.

Systems of opportunity are based on the idea that every person has the capacity to learn, develop, and succeed. Rather than placing restrictions or hurdles on the basis of subjective standards, these settings enable people to reach their greatest potential and make significant contributions to society. They understand that promoting brilliance, innovation, and creativity requires diversity, inclusion, and equity.

Additionally, systems of opportunity give people access to the tools, encouragement, and mentoring they need to succeed. These environments promote opportunities for achievement by providing equal options for education, training, finance, and networking.

They work to break down barriers and provide fair chances for everyone because they understand that while talent is distributed equally, opportunity is not.

Systems of opportunity also promote a culture of ongoing learning and development, where failure is seen as a normal part of the learning process and feedback is highly appreciated. Rather than penalizing errors or setbacks, these settings promote experimentation, taking calculated risks, and perseverance. They recognize that failure is a necessary step toward achievement rather than the end and offer support and direction to help people grow and learn from their experiences.

Systems of opportunity not only offer chances for personal development and accomplishment, but they also promote teamwork and group initiatives. They promote collaboration, teamwork, and mutual support because they understand that no one achieves success alone. Individuals in these settings can maximize their combined abilities and achieve more than they ever could by cooperating to achieve shared objectives.

To sum up, opportunity networks play a crucial role in helping us realize our full potential and accomplish more in life. We can make paths to success for people from all walks of life by establishing conditions that support development, give access to resources and assistance, encourage cooperation and group efforts, and promote a culture of ongoing learning and development. Together, let's construct opportunity systems that enable people to realize their full potential and pave the way for a more promising and just future for all.

RETHINKING EDUCATION: CREATING INSTITUTIONS THAT DEVELOP STUDENTS' UNIQUE SKILLS AND QUALITIES

Education shapes the brains and futures of future generations and is the cornerstone of personal and societal progress. However, consistent curricula and standardized testing sometimes take precedence over the unique skills and characteristics of individual pupils in traditional educational institutions. Rethinking education and creating learning environments that support each student's unique abilities and capabilities are crucial if we are to help every learner reach their full potential.

Rethinking education is moving away from a one-size-fits-all strategy and toward a more individualized, inclusive one that values each student's individual skills and interests. It necessitates redefining education's role from merely dispensing information to enabling people to follow their passions, develop their skills, and reach their greatest potential.

Personalization is a fundamental concept in the construction of schools that foster each student's unique abilities and skills. This entails adjusting the educational process to each student's unique needs, interests, and skill level. With personalized learning, students may go at their own speed, delve deeply into their passions, and investigate subjects that really speak to them. Schools can enable students to take charge of their education and follow routes that fit with their interests and aspirations by giving them options for choice and autonomy.

Creating schools that support each student's unique abilities and strengths calls for a comprehensive approach to education that extends beyond scholastic success, in addition to personalizing.

This entails encouraging social-emotional traits like empathy, fortitude, and teamwork in addition to offering chances for creative expression and experiential learning. Schools may equip students to flourish in a world that is always changing and to make significant contributions to society by developing a well-rounded set of competencies in their pupils.

Establishing a welcoming and inclusive learning environment is another crucial component of building schools that accommodate each student's unique abilities and capabilities. This entails creating an environment where all students feel appreciated and supported—one that values respect, acceptance, and belonging. Schools can accomplish this through offering resources and support services to cater to the individual needs of every student, as well as by encouraging diversity and inclusivity in their policies, staffing, and curriculum. Schools can enable students to actively participate in their education and pursue their interests without fear of discrimination or judgment by fostering a safe and inviting environment.

Rethinking assessment and evaluation procedures to place more emphasis on development and progress than merely grades and test results is also necessary for creating schools that support each student's unique abilities and strengths. This entails measuring student learning and growth through a range of assessment techniques, including projects, portfolios, and performance-based evaluations. Schools can help kids develop a growth mindset and learn from mistakes by giving them constructive criticism and emphasizing progress over perfection.

In order to effectively implement these principles and practices, collaboration and partnership among educators, policymakers, parents, and community members are essential. By working together, stakeholders can identify opportunities for innovation, share best practices, and advocate for policies and resources that support the holistic development of every learner. By building strong partnerships, schools can create a collective vision for education that prioritizes the needs and aspirations of every student and fosters a culture of continuous improvement and excellence.

In conclusion, rethinking education and designing schools that nurture individual talents and strengths are essential for unlocking the hidden potential of every learner. By embracing personalization, holistic development, inclusivity, and collaboration, schools can create learning environments that empower students to discover their passions, cultivate their talents, and thrive in an ever-changing world.

Let's work together to build a future where every student has the opportunity to unleash their full potential and accomplish greater things.

THE UTILIZATION OF COLLECTIVE INTELLIGENCE: HARNESSING THE POTENTIAL OF COLLABORATIVE TEAMWORK

In the quest for achieving higher objectives, individuals frequently encounter a strong inclination towards the efficacy of collaborative efforts. Although individual effort and experience hold value, the collaboration fostered by teamwork can provide exceptional outcomes. Harnessing collective intelligence entails harnessing the varied viewpoints, expertise, and backgrounds of a group to address challenges, produce groundbreaking concepts, and accomplish common objectives.

Collaboration is the fundamental basis for achieving success in various pursuits, be it in professional settings, educational institutions, or local communities. Through the integration of individuals possessing varied backgrounds, knowledge, and viewpoints, teams have the ability to harness collective intelligence in order to address intricate difficulties and attain ambitious objectives that may surpass the capabilities of any individual. Collaboration cultivates ingenuity, originality, and adaptability, while also fostering a feeling of inclusion and collective mission.

One of the primary benefits of team collaboration is the capacity to harness the pooled knowledge and expertise of group members. Every person contributes distinct perspectives, expertise, and backgrounds, which can enhance the process of resolving problems and result in more innovative and efficient solutions. By harnessing the many viewpoints of team members, teams can reveal areas of limited awareness, question preconceived notions, and produce groundbreaking concepts that may not have been achievable through individual endeavors alone.

Moreover, cooperation produces a sense of common ownership as well as responsibility among those working together, resulting in more powerful dedication and determination to achieve shared goals. When individuals work together towards a common aim, they feel a sense of camaraderie and mutual support, which can drive them to overcome difficulties and persevere in the face of challenges. cooperation also encourages learning and progress, as team members have the ability to learn from one another, share best practices, and acquire new abilities through cooperation.

Effective team cooperation requires a supportive and inclusive team culture that values open communication, trust, and respect. Team members should feel empowered to voice their thoughts, share ideas, and challenge assumptions without fear of judgment or punishment. Leaders play a critical role in building a collaborative team culture by defining clear standards, giving chances for cooperation, and recognizing and celebrating team achievements. By fostering a healthy and inclusive team environment, leaders can unlock the full potential of their teams and achieve more success.

Furthermore, excellent communication is vital for successful team collaboration. Team members should communicate honestly and transparently, exchanging information, updates, and comments in a timely way. Clear communication helps guarantee that everyone is on the same page and aligned toward common goals, eliminating misunderstandings and conflicts. In addition to verbal communication, teams can harness technology tools and platforms to promote collaboration and streamline communication, especially in remote or distant teams.

Another crucial part of team collaboration is effective decision-making. Teams often face challenging decisions that require careful analysis and feedback from many viewpoints. By incorporating all team members in the decision-making process and considering a variety of opinions, teams can make more informed and equitable decisions that reflect the collective intelligence of the group. Leaders may promote effective decision-making by building a culture of trust and empowerment, giving guidance and assistance as needed, and ensuring that decisions are founded on evidence and consensus.

In conclusion, using collective intelligence through team cooperation is vital for uncovering hidden potential and accomplishing larger things. By bringing together individuals with varied perspectives, talents, and experiences, teams may handle complex challenges, produce novel ideas, and achieve ambitious goals that may be beyond the reach of any single individual. Effective team collaboration involves a supportive team culture, open communication, inclusive decision-making, and strong leadership. By leveraging the power of team cooperation, people can release their full potential and create exceptional outcomes.

CHAPTER 5

IDENTIFYING AND FOSTERING TALENT

IDENTIFYING HIDDEN POTENTIAL: RECOGNIZING UNTAPPED TALENT DURING INTERVIEWS AND ACADEMIC ADMISSIONS

In today's competitive environment, recognizing latent potential is critical for seizing chances and developing talent. Traditional evaluation techniques frequently emphasize standardized examinations and academic achievements, while ignoring the many abilities, experiences, and qualities that individuals bring to the table.

In this section, we'll look at how important it is to recognize latent talent during interviews and academic admissions, as well as ways to detect hidden potential beyond typical measurements.

Identifying hidden potential begins with acknowledging that talent takes numerous forms and cannot always be captured by standardized methods. While academic achievements are crucial markers of potential, they only paint a partial picture of a person's talents. Other factors, such as creativity, problem-solving abilities, leadership skills, and resilience, are also important and should be evaluated during the evaluation process.

Adopting a comprehensive evaluation strategy is one of the most important tactics for finding hidden potential during interviews and academic admissions. Instead of focusing exclusively on academic transcripts or standardized test results, evaluators should take into account a variety of criteria such as extracurricular activities, volunteer work, internships, personal achievements, and life experiences. Evaluators can obtain a better idea of an individual's unique talents and potential by reviewing their entire background and accomplishments.

Furthermore, evaluators should consider qualitative markers of potential, such as passion, curiosity, desire, and perseverance. These characteristics are sometimes more difficult to define, but they can provide vital information about a person's motivation, desire, and potential for success. By asking probing questions and engaging in meaningful conversations during interviews, evaluators might find hidden abilities and qualities that may not be obvious on paper.

In addition to assessing individual accomplishments and traits, evaluators should analyze the context in which these achievements were produced. For example, someone who overcomes considerable difficulties or adversity to attain academic excellence may exhibit persistence, determination, and resourcefulness, all of which indicate untapped potential. Understanding each applicant's unique circumstances and problems allows evaluators to acquire a more nuanced perspective on their talents and capabilities.

Furthermore, assessors should strive for diversity and representation during the selection process to ensure that all views and viewpoints are heard.

Including people from various backgrounds, cultures, and experiences on interview panels and admissions committees allows evaluators to avoid biases and widen their perception of talent and potential. Diversity promotes creativity, innovation, and quality while also ensuring that latent potential is identified and cultivated, regardless of background or circumstance.

It is also critical for assessors to provide opportunities for applicants to demonstrate their abilities and potential outside of typical evaluation procedures. Portfolio evaluations, creative projects, presentations, or problem-solving exercises are all examples of ways for applicants to demonstrate their talents and abilities in a real-world setting. By providing various assessment options, evaluators can gain a more complete picture of an individual's potential and make more informed conclusions about their admission or employment eligibility.

Finally, ongoing assessment and feedback are critical for unlocking latent potential and assisting individuals in their growth.

Evaluators should provide positive criticism and direction to assist individuals in identifying their strengths and areas for improvement, as well as chances for future development and advancement. By promoting a culture of continual learning and progress, assessors may help individuals realize their full potential and achieve greater success.

Finally, discovering hidden potential during interviews and academic admissions is critical for pursuing opportunities and developing skills. Evaluators can ensure that untapped talent is identified and nurtured regardless of background or circumstance by taking a holistic approach to evaluation, taking qualitative indicators of potential into account, understanding the context of achievements, promoting diversity and representation, providing opportunities for showcasing talents, and providing ongoing assessment and feedback. Let us work together to create a future in which everyone has the opportunity to realize their full potential and achieve great things.

FOSTERING INCLUSIVITY: PROVIDING OPPORTUNITIES FOR EVERYONE TO THRIVE AND SUCCEED

Inclusivity is the foundation of a flourishing society, where everyone has the opportunity to realize their full potential and achieve greater success. However, systemic hurdles and biases frequently prohibit certain groups from fully participating and succeeding in a variety of areas of life. In this section, we'll look at the importance of inclusion and ways to ensure that everyone has the opportunity to grow and prosper.

In order to promote inclusion, systemic barriers and biases that perpetuate inequality and limit opportunities for particular groups must be identified and addressed. This includes barriers based on race, ethnicity, gender, sexual orientation, disability, socioeconomic status, and other characteristics. By removing these barriers and providing a more level playing field, we can ensure that everyone has access to education, jobs, healthcare, and other resources necessary for success.

One of the most important ways to build inclusion is to promote diversity and representation in all parts of society. This involves a diversified representation in leadership roles, decision-making bodies, and media outlets. By ensuring that different voices are heard and acknowledged, we can foster cultures in which everyone feels included, respected, and empowered to share their unique perspectives and abilities.

Furthermore, establishing opportunities for everyone to flourish and prosper necessitates addressing systemic educational disparities. This entails providing equal access to quality education to all students, regardless of background or circumstances. It also entails employing inclusive and culturally responsive teaching approaches that acknowledge and promote the variety of students' experiences, identities, and cultures. By creating a friendly and inclusive learning environment, we can help all children attain their full potential and succeed academically.

In addition to education, encouraging inclusivity entails developing inclusive workplaces that celebrate diversity while promoting equity and inclusion.

This includes putting in place policies and practices that encourage diversity in hiring, retention, and progression, as well as offering training and support to combat unconscious prejudice and promote inclusive leadership. Workplaces that promote inclusivity and belonging may recruit and retain diverse people, generate innovation, and achieve higher success.

Furthermore, providing opportunities for everyone to flourish and achieve necessitates tackling gaps in access to healthcare, housing, and other critical services. This involves ensuring that healthcare services are accessible, cheap, and culturally competent, as well as housing regulations that encourage equal access to secure and affordable housing for all people and families. By addressing these inequities, we may build healthier, more vibrant communities in which everyone can enjoy fulfilling lives.

Another key part of building diversity is providing economic opportunity and empowerment for excluded communities. This includes fostering economic mobility through education, training, and entrepreneurship initiatives, as well as enacting legislation that supports fair wages, worker rights, and economic fairness.

Addressing economic inequality and encouraging economic empowerment will help us build more equitable and resilient societies in which everyone can thrive and flourish.

Finally, promoting inclusivity necessitates continuing commitment and collaboration among individuals, organizations, and communities. It entails confronting preconceptions and biases, pushing for policy changes, and actively trying to foster more inclusive cultures in which everyone feels valued, respected, and supported. By working together, we can make the world more inclusive and equal, allowing everyone to realize their full potential and achieve great things.

To summarize, cultivating inclusion is critical for providing opportunities for everyone to develop and succeed. By addressing systemic barriers and biases, promoting diversity and representation, creating inclusive learning and work environments, addressing disparities in access to essential services, promoting economic opportunity and empowerment, and fostering ongoing commitment and collaboration, we can build a more inclusive and equitable society in which everyone can realize their full potential and achieve great things.

Let us work together to create a future in which everyone may flourish and prosper, regardless of background or circumstances.

BUILDING NETWORKS: CULTIVATING RELATIONSHIPS THAT OPEN DOORS TO NEW OPPORTUNITIES

In today's interconnected world, developing networks and relationships is critical for unlocking hidden potential and capturing new chances. Whether in personal or professional settings, the relationships we make with others can open doors, ignite creativity, and move us forward toward our goals. In this section, we'll look at the value of networking and how to cultivate relationships that lead to greater success and fulfillment.

Building networks entails more than just making contacts; it entails cultivating genuine connections with people who can provide support, direction, and chances for advancement. These relationships can originate from a variety of sources, including coworkers, mentors, peers, friends, family members, and members of professional or social groups.

By cultivating these relationships, we may build a strong support system that will help us overcome obstacles, discover new opportunities, and achieve our goals.

Being proactive and intentional in our relationships with people is one of the most important network-building methods. This includes meeting new people, attending networking events, joining professional associations or social clubs, and engaging in online communities. By putting ourselves out there and developing genuine relationships with others, we may grow our network and create chances for cooperation, mentorship, and mutual support.

Furthermore, establishing networks necessitates authenticity and sincerity in our interactions with people. People are more likely to connect with us and provide help when they believe we are honest, trustworthy, and sincere. Being real and true to ourselves allows us to form meaningful relationships based on mutual respect, understanding, and trust.

Building networks entails not only being proactive and truthful but also investing time and effort in developing long-term relationships.

This includes remaining in touch with contacts, providing support and assistance as needed, and celebrating their accomplishments. We may deepen our relationships and lay the groundwork for collaboration and mutual growth by communicating often and expressing genuine interest in others.

Furthermore, developing networks necessitates being open-minded and responsive to new ideas. Every person we encounter has something significant to offer, whether it's a unique ability, experience, or perspective. By approaching conversations with curiosity and openness, we can learn from one another, widen our horizons, and discover new chances for collaboration and innovation.

Another key part of developing networks is being generous in our relationships with others. This entails providing assistance, guidance, and resources to individuals in our network without expecting anything in exchange.

By sharing our time, knowledge, and contacts, we may foster goodwill and develop our relationships with others, resulting in a supportive community in which everyone can prosper.

Furthermore, developing networks necessitates being proactive in searching out chances for collaboration and partnership. This may include starting initiatives, organizing study groups, or collaborating with people to achieve mutual goals. We can make a bigger impact and accomplish more by leveraging our network's talents and resources.

To summarize, developing networks and fostering relationships is critical for unlocking hidden potential and capturing new possibilities. By being proactive, real, and generous in our contacts with people, we may broaden our network, foster a supportive community, and achieve more success and fulfillment in our personal and professional lives. Let us embrace the power of networking and collaborate to discover our hidden potential and achieve greater success.

CHAPTER 6

ADAPTABILITY AND RESILIENCE

EMBRACING CHANGE AND ADAPTABILITY

NAVIGATING UNCERTAINTY WITH CONFIDENCE

Life will always involve change, and being able to adjust to it is essential to realizing our full potential and achieving greater things. People who accept change with confidence and flexibility are better able to deal with uncertainty, take advantage of new opportunities, and persevere through difficulties in a world that is changing quickly. This part will discuss the value of being flexible and open to change, as well as techniques for confidently navigating uncertain situations.

Whether in our personal lives, our employment, or the environment we live in, change is a constant. We continuously confront new situations and problems that call for us to adapt and change, from changing market trends to unforeseen life catastrophes. Accepting change as a necessary aspect of life and seeing it as a chance for development, education, and self-discovery are two aspects of embracing change.

Accepting change has many advantages, not the least of which being the creation of new chances and possibilities.

We restrict our ability to grow and innovate when we cling to the known or oppose change. But when we welcome change with an open mind and a readiness to adjust, we can find new avenues, unearth latent skills, and accomplish more success than we ever would have imagined.

Furthermore, accepting change encourages resilience and agility, two traits that are necessary for confidently handling ambiguity. Agility is the capacity to swiftly and skillfully adjust to shifting conditions, whereas resilience is the capacity to recover from setbacks and hardship. By developing these traits, we can face adversity head-on and emerge from it stronger, more resilient people who see opportunities to grow and better themselves.

To truly embrace change, we need to cultivate a growth mindset, which is the conviction that our skills and intelligence can be improved with commitment and hard work, in addition to resilience and adaptability. Those with a growth mindset see setbacks as opportunities for learning and development rather than as insurmountable hurdles.

Adopting a growth mindset enables us to face change with optimism and confidence because we know we can adapt and flourish in any circumstance.

Let go of fear and embrace uncertainty with bravery and curiosity in order to fully embrace change. Although uncertainty can be frightening, it also offers chances for investigation, learning, and creativity. We may approach new situations with confidence and joy when we reframe uncertainty as an opportunity to learn and grow, knowing that we have the resilience and adaptability to overcome any problems that may arise.

Maintaining flexibility and an open mind to new opportunities is another crucial component of accepting change. This entails adopting new ways of thinking and being as well as being willing to let go of outdated routines, convictions, and presumptions. By keeping flexible and open-minded, we may adjust to changing situations more easily and grab new possibilities for growth and self-discovery.

Moreover, embracing change includes seeking assistance and direction from others during times of transformation.

Having a solid support network, whether it consists of friends, family, mentors, or coworkers, can offer inspiration, perspective, and useful help when navigating uncertain times.

By reaching out to others and developing a support network, we may handle change with confidence and resilience.

Remaining adaptable and open-minded; and asking for help when needed. Since we can adapt to any circumstance and flourish in it, let's welcome change as a chance for personal development and exploration.

THRIVING IN AMBIGUITY: DEVELOPING THE SKILLS TO NAVIGATE COMPLEX SITUATIONS

In today's fast-paced and ever-changing environment, ambiguity is unavoidable. Whether in our personal or professional lives, we frequently encounter complex and uncertain situations that need us to think on our feet, make difficult decisions, and adapt rapidly to changing circumstances. Thriving in ambiguity is cultivating the skills and mindset required to negotiate uncertainty with confidence and perseverance. In this section, we'll look at why it's important to thrive in uncertainty and how to build the abilities needed to handle challenging scenarios.

Ambiguity is inherent in many facets of life, including navigating job transitions, managing relationships, and making critical life decisions.

Individuals who thrive in ambiguity view it as an opportunity for growth, innovation, and self-discovery rather than a source of anxiety. They approach the unknown with curiosity and confidence, understanding that it presents an opportunity to learn, explore new possibilities, and push their limits.

One of the most important talents for thriving in ambiguity is adaptability—the capacity to change to new conditions and make quick decisions in response to changing scenarios. Adaptability necessitates flexibility, resilience, and a willingness to abandon old ways of thinking and doing things. Individuals who are adaptive may rapidly pivot when confronted with unanticipated problems, seize new possibilities, and turn failures into stepping stones to success.

Furthermore, living in ambiguity necessitates the development of excellent problem-solving skills—the capacity to analyze complex circumstances, identify essential difficulties, and generate innovative solutions. Critical thinking, creativity, and the desire to think outside the box are all necessary for problem-solving. Individuals who succeed at problem-solving may face uncertainty with confidence, knowing they have the skills and ability to overcome whatever problems arise.

In addition to adaptability and problem-solving abilities, success in ambiguity necessitates effective communication and teamwork capabilities. Complex situations frequently necessitate collaboration with others to discover solutions, resolve problems, and attain shared objectives.

Active listening, clear expression of ideas, and the capacity to establish rapport and trust with others are all necessary for effective communication. Teamwork, dispute resolution, and the capacity to work well with people from various backgrounds and perspectives are all examples of collaboration abilities.

Furthermore, thriving in ambiguity entails cultivating emotional intelligence—the ability to comprehend and control our own emotions as well as those of others.

Emotional intelligence enables us to navigate uncertainty through empathy, resilience, and self-awareness. It enables us to remain cool under pressure, form deep bonds with others, and make wise decisions even in difficult circumstances.

Another crucial part of prospering in ambiguity is developing a development mindset—the conviction that our abilities and intelligence can be improved through devotion and effort. Individuals with a growth mentality view setbacks as opportunities for learning and growth, not obstacles to be avoided. They see failure as a normal part of the learning process and view setbacks as opportunities to learn, adapt, and progress.

Furthermore, thriving in ambiguity requires remaining interested and open-minded in the face of uncertainty. Curiosity fuels exploration, discovery, and invention, allowing us to unearth new opportunities and solutions to complicated issues. Maintaining a feeling of curiosity and wonder allows us to negotiate ambiguity with enthusiasm and optimism, knowing that every difficulty is an opportunity for growth and self-discovery.

Finally, thriving amid ambiguity is critical for realizing our full potential and achieving better success in life. We may negotiate challenging situations with confidence, resilience, and grace by honing our flexibility, problem-solving skills, communication, teamwork, emotional intelligence, growth mindset, and curiosity. Let us see uncertainty as a chance for growth and self-discovery, knowing that we possess the abilities and mentality required to succeed in any situation.

EMBRACING DIVERSITY: LEVERAGING DIFFERENCES FOR INNOVATION AND GROWTH

Diversity is a basic component of human society. It includes disparities in color, ethnicity, gender, age, sexual orientation, socioeconomic status, viewpoints, and experiences.

Embracing diversity is more than simply tolerance; it is about appreciating the value that varied viewpoints and experiences bring to the table. In this section, we'll look at why it's important to embrace diversity and how to use differences to drive innovation and growth.

Accepting diversity is critical for realizing untapped potential and fostering innovation and progress. When people from different backgrounds join together, they offer their own perspectives, ideas, and insights, which can lead to groundbreaking inventions and creative solutions to complicated challenges. Organizations that embrace diversity can get access to a greater range of experiences, abilities, and perspectives, resulting in increased creativity and success.

One of the primary advantages of accepting diversity is that it promotes creativity and innovation. When people with diverse experiences and viewpoints work together, they are more likely to produce new ideas and approaches to problem resolution. Diversity fosters creativity by questioning assumptions, fostering unconventional thinking, and stimulating the discovery of new possibilities.

Organizations that embrace diversity may unlock their teams' full potential and propel innovation forward.

Furthermore, embracing variety improves decision-making and problem-solving. When teams are made up of people with different perspectives and experiences, they are more likely to take into account a wider range of factors and points of view when making choices. This can result in more informed, balanced, and effective decision-making, as well as a greater grasp of complicated issues and concerns.

Organizations can make better judgments and achieve more success by using their personnel's diverse backgrounds.

Embracing diversity fosters inclusivity and belonging while also encouraging creativity and innovation. When employees feel valued and recognized for their unique contributions, they are more inclined to fully engage and participate in the workplace. As a result, employee happiness, motivation, and retention improve, as does the company culture. By embracing diversity, organizations may foster an environment in which everyone feels included, valued, and empowered to achieve.

Furthermore, embracing diversity improves organizational performance and competition. Diverse teams outperform homogeneous teams on a variety of metrics, including financial success, customer happiness, and employee engagement. Organizations can acquire a competitive advantage in the marketplace by leveraging the collective knowledge and creativity of diverse teams to achieve greater success in attaining their goals.

Another key part of accepting diversity is developing cultural competency and sensitivity.

This entails gaining an awareness and appreciation for various cultures, traditions, and perspectives, as well as the ability to effectively communicate and work across cultural barriers. Cultural competency encourages empathy, respect, and collaboration among team members, hence increasing trust and strengthening relationships. Organizations may encourage cultural competence, resulting in a more inclusive and peaceful work environment in which everyone can prosper.

Furthermore, embracing diversity necessitates intentional measures to combat unconscious bias and promote fairness and inclusion.

This includes putting in place rules and practices that encourage diversity in recruiting, retention, and progression, as well as offering training and education to enhance awareness of unconscious bias and promote inclusive behaviors. Organizations may level the playing field by eliminating bias and encouraging equity, ensuring that everyone has an equal opportunity to succeed based on their skills, abilities, and contributions.

To summarize, embracing diversity is critical for unlocking latent potential and accelerating innovation and progress.

Organizations can benefit from team diversity by encouraging creativity, improving decision-making, promoting inclusivity, improving organizational performance, creating cultural competence, and resolving unconscious bias. Let us embrace diversity as a source of strength and inspiration, knowing that it holds the key to unlocking our untapped potential and achieving greater success.

BUILDING RESILIENCE: BOUNCING BACK STRONGER FROM ADVERSITY

Resilience is the ability to adapt and recover in the face of adversity, obstacles, or major sources of stress. It is not about avoiding obstacles, but about confronting them full-on, learning from them, and emerging stronger than before. Resilience is an important characteristic that can help people overcome hurdles and thrive in the face of uncertainty on their path to self-discovery and success. In this section, we'll look at the importance of developing resilience and ways for overcoming hardship.

Building resilience is critical for discovering untapped potential and achieving better success in life. Adversity is an unavoidable aspect of life, and how we respond to it has a significant impact on our capacity to achieve our goals and fulfill our potential. Individuals who are resilient are better able to negotiate challenges, endure disappointments, and continue pursuing their dreams. Individuals who develop resilience can recover stronger from hardship, emerging more resilient, confident, and capable of attaining their goals.

One of the most important components of resilience is a strong sense of self-worth and confidence in one's talents. Resilient people trust in their ability to overcome obstacles and achieve their goals, especially in the face of setbacks or failure. This self-belief motivates and drives people to endure in the face of hardship, rather than giving up or succumbing to despair.

Furthermore, increasing resilience entails learning appropriate coping mechanisms for dealing with stress and adversity. This includes practicing good habits like regular exercise, meditation, and mindfulness, as well as seeking social support from friends, family, or professional networks. These coping skills help people develop resilience by encouraging emotional well-being, lowering stress, and improving their ability to deal with stressful situations.

Building resilience entails not just establishing coping techniques, but also framing obstacles as opportunities for development and learning. Setbacks and failures are viewed as useful learning experiences by resilient people, who use them to build new abilities, gain insight into their own strengths and shortcomings, and evolve as individuals.

Instead of concentrating on past mistakes or losses, they seek answers and move forward with newfound determination and resilience.

Furthermore, developing resilience necessitates establishing a positive perspective and approach to adversity. Resilient people may keep a good attitude in the face of adversity, viewing hardships as transitory setbacks rather than insurmountable obstacles. This optimistic thinking allows individuals to remain focused, motivated, and resilient in the pursuit of their goals, even in the face of adversity or disappointments.

Another crucial part of resilience development is cultivating social support and connections with others. Resilient people have strong support networks that include friends, family, mentors, and peers who offer encouragement, advice, and emotional support during challenging times. These social relationships help people feel less alienated and more supported, which boosts their resilience and ability to recover from hardship.

Furthermore, improving problem-solving skills and the ability to adapt to changing situations are essential components of resilience building. Individuals who are resilient are inventive and innovative in problem-solving, as well as flexible and adaptable when confronted with difficulty. This adaptability enables individuals to face uncertainty and conquer hurdles with confidence and resilience.

In conclusion, developing resilience is critical for unleashing latent potential and achieving better success in life. Individuals can overcome adversity by gaining self-belief, effective coping mechanisms, a positive mindset, social support, problem-solving abilities, and adaptability, allowing them to emerge stronger, more resilient, and capable of attaining their goals. Let us recognize resilience as a useful quality that may help us overcome obstacles and thrive in the face of adversity, knowing that it holds the key to unlocking our latent potential and achieving greater success.

LEADING WITH EMPATHY: UNDERSTANDING AND VALUING DIFFERENT PERSPECTIVES

In today's interconnected world, successful leadership demands more than technical expertise and strategic thought. It necessitates empathy—the ability to comprehend and relate to the thoughts, feelings, and experiences of others. Leading with empathy is not only being compassionate and understanding but also acknowledging and appreciating the various viewpoints and experiences that each individual brings to the table. In this section, we'll look at the value of empathy in leadership, as well as tactics for understanding and valuing diverse perspectives.

Empathy-driven leadership is critical for uncovering latent potential and encouraging collaboration, creativity, and growth. Empathetic leaders foster an inclusive environment in which everyone feels heard, appreciated, and respected. They foster trust, strengthen relationships, and motivate others to bring their best selves to the table. Individuals who lead with empathy can help their teams realize their full potential and achieve better success.

One of the primary advantages of leading with empathy is that it promotes understanding and connection among team members.

When leaders display empathy for others, they foster a safe and supportive environment in which people can share their thoughts, concerns, and ideas. Open communication creates trust and collaboration, which leads to increased team cohesion and innovation.

Furthermore, leading with empathy encourages diversity and inclusion by acknowledging and valuing each person's unique viewpoints and experiences. Empathetic leaders recognize the value of variety and actively seek out other perspectives and ideas to help them make decisions and solve problems. By embracing diversity and inclusion, leaders may tap into their teams' combined expertise and creativity, resulting in more inventive and successful outcomes.

Empathy-based leadership promotes understanding and inclusivity while also increasing employee engagement and happiness. When leaders display empathy for their team members, it demonstrates that they care about their well-being and are invested in their success.

This fosters a pleasant work atmosphere in which employees feel driven, encouraged, and respected, resulting in better job satisfaction and commitment.

Furthermore, empathy-based leadership promotes resilience and improves conflict resolution. Empathetic leaders can better grasp the underlying motivations and emotions that drive conflicts and disagreements, helping them to develop constructive solutions that address the basic causes of the problem. Leaders may develop an environment of trust and collaboration by encouraging open communication and empathy, resulting in peaceful conflict resolution and stronger connections.

Leading with empathy also entails exhibiting humility and vulnerability as a leader. Empathetic leaders are prepared to recognize when they don't know the solutions and seek input and feedback from others. They are willing to learn from their mistakes, take risks, and attempt new techniques. Leaders who demonstrate humility and vulnerability foster an environment in which team members feel comfortable sharing their own thoughts and viewpoints, resulting in increased creativity and innovation.

Furthermore, leading with empathy entails actively listening to others and striving to understand their viewpoints without passing judgment or bias.

Empathetic leaders conduct active listening by paying close attention to the speaker, asking clarifying questions, and summarizing their understanding to ensure clarity. Leaders may foster trust and rapport by actually listening to and valuing the viewpoints of others, resulting in better connections and more successful collaboration.

Finally, leading with empathy is critical for realizing hidden potential and attaining better success as a leader. Leaders can foster understanding and connection, promote diversity and inclusion, increase employee engagement and satisfaction, build resilience, effectively navigate conflicts, demonstrate humility and vulnerability, and practice active listening to create inclusive and supportive environments in which everyone can thrive. Let us embrace empathy as a powerful leadership tool that can help us unlock our teams' collective potential and achieve greater success together.

CONTINUOUSLY EVOLVING AND GROWING IN A RAPIDLY CHANGING WORLD

In a world characterized by rapid technology breakthroughs, altering societal standards, and changing industries, the pursuit of knowledge and personal growth is more important than ever. Lifelong learning is not a luxury; it is essential for being relevant, adaptive, and fulfilled in both personal and professional settings. In this section, we'll look at the value of lifelong learning and how to consistently evolve and improve in a quickly changing world.

Accepting lifelong learning is critical for discovering hidden potential and achieving better success in life. Individuals who pursue lifelong learning can stay ahead of the curve, adapt to new obstacles, and capitalize on emerging possibilities. Individuals who commit to ongoing growth and development can realize their full potential and reach new heights of achievement and fulfillment.

One of the primary advantages of embracing lifelong learning is that it promotes adaptation and resilience in the face of change.

Lifelong learners are better able to overcome uncertainty and ambiguity because they possess the skills and information required to adapt to new conditions and obstacles. Lifelong learners may be adaptable and resilient in the face of fast change by constantly updating their skills and keeping up with industry trends.

Furthermore, lifelong learning fosters personal and professional development by increasing individuals' horizons and viewpoints. Lifelong learners can gain new insights, encourage creativity, and build a deeper awareness of themselves and their surroundings by being exposed to new ideas, experiences, and ways of thinking. Lifelong learning is more than just learning new skills; it's also about cultivating a growth mindset and a passion for information, which promotes constant improvement and self-discovery.

In addition to fostering personal and professional development, lifelong learning improves job possibilities and advancement. Employers in today's knowledge-based economy value those who are willing to learn and grow.

Lifelong learners are more likely to remain relevant and competitive in the labor market because they possess the skills and information required to adapt to changing work requirements and industry needs. Individuals who invest in their own learning and development can discover new employment prospects and achieve better success in their chosen sector.

Furthermore, lifelong learning promotes innovation and creativity by encouraging people to try new things and experiment with alternative methods. Lifelong learners are more inclined to think outside the box, question the current quo, and develop novel solutions to challenging challenges. Lifelong learning, by cultivating a culture of curiosity and experimentation, may promote innovation and propel businesses forward in today's quickly evolving environment.

Another advantage of adopting lifelong learning is that it fosters personal contentment and well-being. Lifelong learners are more likely to find meaning and fulfillment in their lives because they are always growing, evolving, and following their passions. Lifelong learners can improve their happiness, fulfillment, and overall well-being by engaging in mentally stimulating and challenging activities.

Furthermore, lifelong learning promotes social relationships and community participation by allowing individuals to connect with others who share their interests and passions.

Lifelong learners frequently participate in learning communities, workshops, and seminars where they can share ideas, work together on projects, and form meaningful relationships. Lifelong learning can improve people's sense of belonging and connection to others by encouraging social ties and community participation, resulting in increased happiness and well-being.

To summarize, embracing lifelong learning is critical for realizing latent potential and achieving more success and joy in life. Lifelong learning enables individuals to thrive in today's rapidly changing world by fostering adaptability and resilience, encouraging personal and professional growth, increasing career opportunities and advancement, driving innovation and creativity, promoting personal fulfillment and well-being, and fostering social connections and community engagement. Let's embrace lifelong learning as a lifelong path of growth, discovery, and fulfillment, knowing that it holds the key to unlocking our latent potential and doing greater things.

CONCLUSION

In conclusion, "Unlock Your Hidden Potential" is a transformative guide that illuminates the path to self-discovery and empowers readers to achieve greatness. Accepting the ideas presented in this book will set you on the path to self-improvement and enable you to reach your full potential. You will learn the secrets of achieving more and leading a happy life via self-awareness, tenacity, and the application of useful techniques. I hope this book encourages you to see the beauty in yourself, to believe in yourself enough to follow your aspirations no matter what, and to realize the tremendous potential you have inside you.